THE HISTORY OF CURRICULUM IN AMERICAN SCHOOLS

FROM THE PILGRIMS TO THE PRESENT

ANGELA HODGES EDGAR, ED.D.

authorHOUSE®

AuthorHouse™
1663 Liberty Drive, Suite 200
Bloomington, IN 47403
www.authorhouse.com
Phone: 1-800-839-8640

First published by AuthorHouse 3/12/2009

ISBN: 978-1-4389-5775-3 (sc)

*Printed in the United States of America
Bloomington, Indiana*

This book is printed on acid-free paper.

PREFACE

Educators today find themselves discussing what schools should teach, just as educators in the past. This topic has existed as long as schools. Curriculum has been an important topic for centuries. Confucius became the first private teacher in history around 561 B.C. In the 1st century A.D., Quintilian, a Roman educator, wrote that students ought to be able to study what interests them. Plato, a Greek philosopher from the fourth century B.C., believed that a person's knowledge is innate, and all a teacher needs to do is help the person recall the inborn knowledge and ideas.

While today's public schools scarcely resemble their colonial beginnings, many of our current controversies are rooted in the past. We continue to dispute the role of religion in schools, the differences in state government education policies, and the inequities in educational opportunities for women, people of color, and the poor.

This book tracks the curriculum changes throughout history, starting from the colonial beginnings in the seventeenth century to the present curriculum debates with the No Child Left Behind Act. Throughout these centuries, people have debated how to educate American children. Curricula have come and gone, only to reappear decades later. The important educational ideas and events of each century will be evident in this book, thus showing that not much has changed in the American educational system since the Pilgrims landed at Plymouth Rock. America still cannot agree on how to best teach children, which produces endless curriculum wars.

Table of Contents

CHAPTER 1

COLONIAL BEGINNINGS IN THE SEVENTEENTH CENTURY

Education in America took root with the Pilgrims' landing at Plymouth Rock in the early 1600s. In the earliest days of America, the Bible was the curriculum for teaching its stories and to elicit a good, moral life. All Puritans had an ultimate goal of a strong union with God that gave assurance of salvation. The Puritans felt that this could only occur from long hours of spiritual and intellectual exercises, such as going to church and reading the Bible. People who were educated were perceived to be the ones who attained a state of grace, and those who were unlearned were damned to be tormented by hell fire.

Education in the seventeenth century was private and predominately religious. It was patterned after the English model. Education originally developed as a two-track system with people from the lower classes receiving minimal instruction and only learning to read, write, calculate, and receive religious instruction. The upper classes were allowed to pursue an education beyond the basics. Religion could not be easily separated from academics during this time of settlement and construction. It was the thread that held communities together that struggled during the early years of hardship. The religious and moral education of youth was the most important factor in early American schools. The first book in the classroom was the Bible. It was central to a child's education for its content and the way it was used to build skills. Students learned how to read using the Bible. Much of the school day was spent memorizing and reciting scriptures from it, and passages were copied to learn penmanship.

Children aged six through eight attended a dame school, where a lady in the neighborhood, called a dame, would teach letters, numbers, and prayers as she did her daily household chores. A modest fee was charged to those who attended. Attendance was dependent on the season and work at home that needed to be done. For most females, the dame school provided their only education. The hornbook, a wooden paddle with parchment pasted on, was one of the first tools used to teach reading. Letters, numbers, and Bible verses such as the Lord's Prayer were sometimes written on the parchment with ink and quill. The paper would then be glued to the board. To keep the paper from being destroyed, a layer of horn was placed over the top.

The printing press, which allowed the expansion of printed materials, was invented in this century. This is what brought about textbooks. The printing press was a less expensive type-face that reduced the cost of production.

The first textbook was the *New England Primer*, which was published between 1688 and 1690 by Benjamin

Harris. The ninety-page work contained religious maxims, woodcuts, alphabet assistants, acronyms, catechisms, and moral lessons. This text was full of religious doctrine, and became the most widely used textbook in the colonies for over a hundred years. For those students who advanced beyond the hornbook, or *Primer*, the Bible, the Testament, and the Psalter became the textbooks for instruction.

The Puritans formed the first formal secondary school in 1635. It was called the Roxbury Latin School. These Latin Grammar Schools were originally designed for only sons of certain social classes who were going to be leaders in the church, state, or courts. The study of Latin and Greek and literature was blended with the Protestant religion. Girls were not considered for these schools, because all of the world leaders were males from the upper social class. The Latin Grammar Schools taught reading, writing, and arithmetic. The purpose was to prepare boys for the entrance exam for Harvard College, which was the first American college. Harvard was established in 1636, and was named after John Harvard, who was the only instructor of nine students when the college first opened. The purpose of Harvard was to raise a literate and devout clergy through a knowledge of God and Jesus Christ. Harvard students read Bible scriptures two times a day and attended lectures and tutoring sessions.

Massachusetts was in the forefront of educational reform when a law was enacted in 1642 that stated any child not being properly educated would have to be apprenticed to a trade. Virginia had a similar law in 1646. It stated that parents of children who had been apprenticed to them were responsible for their basic education and literacy. The governing officials stated that all children and servants should be able to demonstrate competency in reading and writing. This was so that everyone would be able to understand and abide by the governing laws of the land. The law stated that if the parents did not show proper responsibility in educating their children, and they were not able to meet basic criteria, it would be the government's right to remove the children from the home and place them where they could receive adequate instruction.

An early form of education in the American colonies was apprenticeship. There was a great need for skilled workers due to the influx of new immigrants. The new world was wealthy with raw materials which needed many people to develop. Apprenticeship was on-the-job training which was based on ancient and medieval practices. England systemized the training. The Poor Law was transferred to the American colonies in 1601. Eventually, Massachusetts and Virginia passed laws in favor of this educational endeavor.

After young boys completed their education at the dame school, they were able to read. The curriculum allowed limited math and writing skills. At about age nine, the boys' parents chose for them one of three options. They could attend a Latin School, which had college prep courses. Most did not go on to college, since at that time, the curriculum was only for the training of ministers. A second choice was for the boys to be trained at home for the occupation of their father. A third option was apprenticeship, which sometimes required monthly payments to the craftsman who was the employer. Apprenticeship gave the craftsman much-needed help in his work, and the children gained experiences that would prepare them to continue skills of business in the future.

Schools were not entirely tax-supported. They were usually financed by a combination of general town taxes, tuition payments made by parents, and donations of fuel. The requirement that these parents pay part of the tuition for elementary schooling meant that the children of the poorer parents might not receive as much schooling as the children of the more affluent. Education was mostly informal for poor white children. Boys usually learned to hunt, fish, or farm from their fathers. Girls learned to cook and sew from their mothers. There was minimal schooling in the backwoods areas. The colonists felt that the children of workers and peasants should have a minimal primary education, which consisted of reading, writing, arithmetic, and religion.

The black slaves were trained to work in the fields, tend livestock, blacksmith, or to be mill hands. Some were butlers, maids, and coachmen. They were considered to be the top of the slave society. Most slaves were not taught to read or write. Some masters, however, taught their slaves to be literate. Formal education was forbidden for slaves in most of the South.

The Law of 1647, known as the Old Deluder Satan Act, was born out of parental negligence. It was at this point in history that formal schooling became more desirable. This law required that towns of fifty families have an elementary school and hire a schoolmaster who would teach children to read and write. Towns with one hundred families must have a Latin Grammar School and hire a schoolmaster who could prepare children to attend Harvard College. Teachers were being formally hired for the sole purpose of teaching the nation's youth. They were paid to teach either by the government or individual parents. School was becoming more of a priority. There were some teachers who were called traveling schoolmasters who went to various towns to teach children. The colonial teachers were men, with the exception of the women who taught in dame schools. The town school teacher was not as highly educated or thought of as the master who taught in the Latin Grammar School.

The colonial mode of education emphasized parental responsibility and limited government role. Education took place in the family, the church, the school, and the workplace. Schooling was non-compulsory, supported by a combination of funding sources, and characterized by brief terms and unequal access. Scattered population made formal schooling more difficult and less important in the South and on the frontier.

The concept of education reform was alive in the seventeenth century. Educators developed new ways of thinking about education. Many of these ideas were born in Britain and carried over to America during the 1600s. This was a time of people striving for more knowledge. The belief was that with this gain of knowledge came power. Educated people had power of mind, power of self, and power of country.

Chapter 2

Curriculum in the Colonies in the Eighteenth Century

The elementary curriculum continued to be centered around religious indoctrination. The church-supported schools consisted mainly of reading, religion, and morals. Some attention was given to writing and arithmetic. The principal textbooks of instruction continued to be the Bible, the Testament, and the Psalter. However, there was an interest in science during the eighteenth century. Religion did not stop being an important force at this time, but the drift toward a natural theology in some circles made it possible for the school curriculum to free itself from the tight grip of religion.

The curriculum in the Latin Grammar Schools continued to focus on college preparatory studies of the ancient languages and literatures, but now the purpose of this study became much less religious and more oriented toward producing the cultured gentleman and scholar. As families grew in wealth, they wanted a higher social standing. Refined speech; gracious manners; and familiarity with Latin, Greek, and classical authors was required to reach this higher social standing. Since the Latin Grammar Schools were bound by college entrance requirements and tradition, they were unable and unwilling to adapt to the more practical needs for arithmetic, accounting, and bookkeeping.

Out of this dilemma, a new kind of secondary school was established, which was called the Academy. The Academy was typically a private boarding school. Benjamin Franklin is credited with starting the first Academy in Philadelphia in 1751. Franklin's concept of an academy of learning consisted of a curriculum much like the Latin Grammar School combined with a more practical curriculum that offered accounting, bookkeeping, and mathematics. There were two parallel courses of study offered, which were the Latin and the English. The Latin master, or teacher, had a title, and the English had none. The Latin teacher made twice the salary, but the English teacher had twice the number of students in class.

The purpose of college and the method of instruction continued through the eighteenth century. Most colleges were founded through sectarian leadership, but their broad focus was through a classical curriculum to guard against ignorance and to impart useful knowledge. In addition to preparing men for ministry, colleges were preparing them to be lawyers and statesmen for the colonies. Latin, Greek, logic, rhetoric, and grammar instruction made up the classical curriculum in colleges at this time.

Protestants believed that education should be for everyone. For the first time in America, the masses were putting pressure on the institutions to adapt the college curriculum so that the average person could be educated.

Less extensive Latin and Greek was wanted, as well as more preparation for a common profession. During the Great Awakening of the 1740s, student uprisings were occurring at colonial colleges against the traditional classical curriculum that was believed to only be suitable for ministers and lawyers. However, the elite families and civic leaders were not pressuring the colleges to change in order to provide the less fortunate with an opportunity for a college education. That would mean competition for knowledge, jobs, and wealth.

Females received little or no formal education at this time. Most were educated at home. Girls occasionally attended dame schools. However, times were changing. Sarah Pierce established the Litchfield Female Academy in 1792. In the beginning, only two students attended. The attendance eventually grew to 140 students. Almost 3,000 females were educated at this academy, which is extraordinary since formal education in secondary schools and colleges was reserved for males.

A shift in the form of governance in the colonies was going on in this century. The colonists wanted democracy instead of the aristocracy that was found in England. The opposing pulls from the old country and the new world had an impact on higher education. People who favored the classical curriculum were probably fighting an inner conflict over loyalty to their homeland traditions in England. Wanting the new democracy called into question these loyalties, which urged educators to rethink what education would be in a free society. Therefore, innovative ideas such as instruction in the vernacular arose, as well as a shift away from Latin and Greek courses. Since there was a steady increase in textbooks in the vernacular after 1750, college professors were better equipped to offer a different education.

A standard curriculum was difficult to achieve in the large and sparsely populated new country. One way to try and promote a curriculum that advocated democracy and independence from England was the development of textbooks. Noah Webster introduced the Blue Back Speller in 1783. This book emphasized patriotic and moral values as well as grammar and spelling.

The new national government passed the Land Ordinance of 1785, which set aside a portion of every township in the unincorporated territories of the United States for use in education. The United States Constitution was written in 1787. Education was left out of the Constitution, which left Americans without direction on the issue. At the time, education, particularly higher education, was for the social elite. Addressing education in the Constitution might have seemed provocative to the colonists. By leaving education out of this document, the writers were giving more power to the states. The founding fathers supported education, which showed by the passing of the Land Ordinance of 1785, which set aside a portion of land in the unincorporated territories of the United States for establishing schools and colleges.

CHAPTER 3

CURRICULUM IN THE COLONIES IN THE NINETEENTH CENTURY

The public school as we know it began in the mid-nineteenth century. Its founders called it the common school. As leader of the common school movement, Horace Mann is sometimes called the father of the public school. Common schools were funded by local property taxes. In Massachusetts in 1827, there was no tuition charged, and the schools were open to all white children. Common schools encouraged shared values and loyalties to America. These schools were to homogenize and discipline the population to produce intelligent citizens and to disseminate a common culture. By 1870, every state provided free elementary education.

Since the Constitution omitted any mention of education as a federal responsibility, the issue was left to the states as each state government set up its own policy, practice, and means of funding schools. There was a small amount of state regulation on common schools. Although the states made the local districts responsible for implementing their policies, the districts got their powers

11

from the state. Local school districts could control their affairs only by permission from the state legislatures.

After the American Revolution, the general pattern of school control remained localized and decentralized in most of the northern states. An emphasis was placed on education. Common schools were governed by local school committees. The school district had its own elected school board. They were supported partially by property taxes and partially by parental tuition payments. In the cities, inexpensive pay schools were supplemented by a number of charity schools operated by churches and nondenominational societies. The Midwestern and other northern states mostly adopted the New England pattern of township or district control. The southern states adopted the county as their unit of educational administration.

More girls participating in education increased school attendance. Female academies grew during this period, furthering the notion of females' intellectual capability. Teaching swung from being a male profession to being predominately female at the elementary level, partly because of the changing attitudes about women and also because town officials paid female teachers lower wages.

In the nineteenth century, the American classroom was sparsely decorated and furnished. The classroom was simple and had few resources. In the one-room schoolhouse, students of all ages and abilities were present. The sole teacher was usually an unmarried woman. The most basic resources used were: slate, chalk, and a few books. Teaching and learning consisted mainly of literacy, penmanship, arithmetic, and good manners. Recitation, drilling, and oral quizzes at the end of the day were the norm in classrooms across America.

Tests and quizzes were common in nineteenth century schools. Teachers would often measure student knowledge by requiring students to stand up and take an oral quiz at the end of the school day. The first standard test of major significance was introduced in the 1870s. This was the two-day exam called the Eighth Grade Examination, which students from rural schools were required to pass in order to attend high school.

Massachusetts enacted the Compulsory Attendance Act of 1852. This law included mandatory attendance for children between the ages of eight and fourteen for at least three months out of the year. Six weeks had to be consecutive out of the three months. There were exceptions to the attendance law, which were: the child attended another school for the same amount of time, proof was provided that the child had already learned the subjects, poverty, and physical or mental ability of the child was so that he could not attend school. Penalty for not sending a child to school was a fine of up to $20.00, and the violators were to be prosecuted by the city. The local school committee could not enforce the law, so it was ineffective. However, the law did keep the importance of school before the public and increased public opinion in favor of education.

In 1873, the compulsory attendance law was revised. The age limit was reduced to twelve, but the annual attendance was increased to twenty weeks each year. There was also enforcement established by forming jurisdictions for prosecution and the hiring of truant officers. Some of our current laws have taken root from these early laws and have expanded on them.

By 1865, the church-dominated reading and writing schools had been replaced by an eight-year graded elementary school that had a more intensive and expanded curriculum. More children were attending school. In the nineteenth century, democratization, industrial development, and nationalism converged to reshape the school curriculum. The first kindergarten was also started in this century.

The economy in the colonies had been mainly agrarian. As the nineteenth century progressed, waterways were increasingly used as a source of power and as a way for transportation. There was a rapid extension of communication following the invention of the telegraph. The development of railroads facilitated transportation. The invention of the steam engine made more power available. Industrial capitalism was not to come of age until the second half of the century, but it was beginning to change the lives of the Americans.

In the nineteenth century, the flag became a symbol of common allegiance. Patriotic songs were being written, and monuments such as the one at Bunker Hill were being erected. Historic people, such as Washington, were transformed into national heroes. By the middle of the nineteenth century, patriotism was strong. This national feeling had a substantial impact on the content of the school curriculum.

In the elementary curriculum, the religious motive came to be channeled into what was called moral and character development. The elementary readers contained a good deal of moralistic content. Another aim of the elementary curriculum was universal literacy. This aim developed from the democratization that occurred as a result of independence and the frontier movement. Literacy had once been important for religious reasons such as reading the Bible, but it now became an ideal based on the assumption that it furthered freedom for people. Out of democratization came the American value of individual success. While individual success was promoted in much of the elementary curriculum, it was more typically found in the secondary schools at this time. Democratization promised upward economic and social mobility for children of the common man. The third aim of the elementary curriculum was citizenship. This came out of the rise of nationalism following the Revolution and the War of 1812. The early readers and the addition of American geography and history to the curriculum is evidence of the concern for the training of loyal and responsible citizens.

Vocational or practical competence was important for producing responsible citizens. This aim was more evident at the secondary level, but it was manifested in the increased emphasis on arithmetic at the elementary level. Vocational competence had its roots in the industrial development that was occurring during this century.

Mental discipline was emerging as a curriculum aim. It was less evident in the elementary curricula. Mental discipline stressed the importance of training the mind as opposed to the acquisition of knowledge. Math was taught as an exercise that would strengthen the reasoning powers of the mind. At the elementary level, arithmetic and English grammar were taught for this purpose.

At the elementary level, the curriculum stressed moral and character development, universal literacy, and responsible citizenship. At the same time, it laid the foundation for what was going to be emphasized in the secondary level, which was individual success, vocational or practical competence, and mental discipline.

Reading was important in the elementary curriculum. The popularity of *The New England Primer* was decreasing, but it was still used. The Bible continued to be used as a resource for teaching reading in the nineteenth century. *The First Part of a Grammatical Institute of the English Language*, familiarly known as *The Blue Back Speller*, was published in 1782 by Noah Webster. It is credited with establishing spelling as a separate subject in the elementary curriculum and with popularizing the spelling bee in America.

The most popular schoolbook in the nineteenth century was the *McGuffey Reader*, which was introduced in 1836. The *McGuffey Readers* were a set of six books, which increased in difficulty. They were based on world literature, and were the basis for teaching literacy as well as the basic values such as honesty and charity. These readers gave the teacher flexibility to teach students of different ages and levels. The McGuffey First and Second Readers appeared in 1836, and the Third and Fourth in 1837. This was when the first graded readers appeared.

Writing became more important in the elementary curriculum as the availability of paper and ink increased. The ability to write was seen more as a practical necessity than it was in earlier years. Reading and writing taken together gained support from the aims of universal literacy and responsible citizenship.

After the publication of graded textbooks, arithmetic became firmly established in the elementary curriculum. Earlier in the nineteenth century, arithmetic was taught mainly for its practical value, but later in the century, it was valued more for its mental discipline function. By the middle of the nineteenth century, arithmetic was vying with English grammar for first place in the elementary curriculum.

Geography became a fixed subject in the elementary curriculum by the Civil War. Geography textbooks contained a question and answer format and concentrated on the geography of the United States. Maps as learning aids were rare. American history did not become a separate subject in the elementary curriculum until the latter part of the nineteenth century. Earlier in the century, however, historical material appeared in the readers.

At the secondary level, the curriculum aims were much the same as the elementary. The universal literacy aim of the elementary curriculum was not a factor in secondary curricula. However, moral and character training was important. Training loyal and responsible citizens was important at the secondary level, as well as vocational and practical competence. The individual success motive and the mental discipline theory both shaped the secondary curricula at this time.

The Boston Latin School introduced arithmetic into its curriculum after 1814. The traditional classical Latin Grammar School only feebly responded to the growing American demands for a broader curriculum. As a consequence, these schools continually declined in importance throughout this time period.

The Academies continued to grow during the first half of the nineteenth century. These schools were indicative of the democratization process that was taking place in America. The Academy brought about opportunity for secondary education to American middle class students. Because the curriculum of the Academies met the varying needs of diverse constituencies, they became the dominant secondary schools in America by the middle of the nineteenth century.

As the Civil War approached, most Academies offered the traditional college preparatory curriculum, such as Latin, Greek, and arithmetic. These subjects became viewed as vehicles of mental discipline. In the English department, English grammar continued to be most important. This subject satisfied the values of practical competence and individual social success by fostering elegance in speech and writing.

Democratization and individual success during this time made training in public speaking a necessity. As a result, many Academies offered courses in rhetoric and declamation. These subjects later turned into the modern-day courses in English composition. Masterpieces of English authors were read, and these works appeared in advanced readers. English literature textbooks did not appear until after the Civil War.

The patriotism developed geography and history in the Academies. Growing nationalism and the aim for citizenship were responsible for introducing the study of American political documents, such as the Declaration of Independence and the Constitution. This area of instruction was conducted with almost the same fervor as religious materials had been earlier. These early precursors of modern civics courses usually were closely associated with the study of history.

The role of science in the promotion of industrialization during the nineteenth century brought about the introduction of natural philosophy into the curriculum. Sciences, such as chemistry, astronomy, and botany also were being introduced. All of these sciences were taught from the textbook. It was not until the middle of the century that experiments conducted by the teacher were being introduced. After the Civil War, physics became part of the curriculum.

Arithmetic in the Academy served the purposes of practical competence and mental discipline. Geometry, because of its practical application in surveying, was taught in the Academies from an early date. However, algebra did not make much headway until the nineteenth century. Algebra was required for entrance to Harvard in 1820, and geometry was first required in 1844.

Modern languages were taught from an early date in Academies for use in international trade. They were taught both for practical reasons and for cultural improvement. French was immensely popular as a cultural subject and was considered a necessary accomplishment for well-bred youth. After 1830, German was gaining popularity because of the interest in science.

When the public high school developed in the mid-nineteenth century, offering the English curriculum free to all students, the Academy declined. High school, originally known as the English Classical School, came into existence in 1821 in Boston. Its name was changed to the English High School in 1824. It was for boys who were twelve years and older. This high school, like many others that followed, was intended to provide education beyond the elementary level at public expense for the children of parents who could not afford to pay the tuition at the Academy.

In the 1870s, there were court cases, such as Michigan's Kalamazoo case in 1874, that ruled that school districts could establish and support public high schools with tax funds. By the years 1889-1890, there were 2,526 public high schools in the United States that were enrolling 202,063 students. There were 1,632 private academies that enrolled 94,391 students.

The curriculum of the early high schools was very similar to that of the Academies. English grammar, arithmetic, geography, history, and bookkeeping were the basic subjects offered. Many early high schools also offered algebra, natural philosophy, moral philosophy, and criticisms of English authors. Languages other than English were not taught in the Boston English Classical School at first, but high schools very early came to offer the college preparatory subjects of Latin and Greek.

The Massachusetts Law of 1827 required that a high school be established in every town of 500 families or more and that these high schools offer United States history, bookkeeping, algebra, geometry, and surveying. High schools in towns having 4,000 or more people were required to add to the core curriculum the subjects of Greek, Latin, history, rhetoric, and logic. By the time of the Civil War, 300 high schools had been established across the United States. By this time, their curricula were becoming increasingly different from the curricula of the Academy.

From 1830 to 1850, more than one million Catholic immigrants came to the eastern seaboard of the United States settling in the large urban areas where work could be found and housing was available. Once these new families settled, prejudice against them was evident. Religion was a focal point of education in this period, and the Protestants were in control. The public schools focused on assimilation. The public schools used the King James translation of the Bible, which the Catholics strongly rejected. Catholics did not accept the teachings of the Protestant church or schools. They believed that education of their children would be most prosperous with the use of Catholic type bibles and prayers. The Catholics' request for the use of their own bible and prayers in the public school was denied. The Catholic children were forced to become Protestant if they were to be educated in the public schools. The development of a parochial school system became necessary, and this led to the private Catholic school system.

As population increased and schools started to provide more services, it was clear that there was a need for more teachers to help carry out the teaching and clerical duties. These changes came along in the middle of the nineteenth century. The original principal was actually called a principal teacher. A principal teacher was required to fulfill many roles in the community. They were the teachers, town clerks, grave diggers, church chorus leaders, court messengers, and sometimes the church bell ringers. The concept of a principal teacher started at the high school level and eventually caught on at the primary level of education. Eventually, the teaching and other duties that were required became too time consuming and the principal concentrated only on managing the schools. Educational administration was brought about in the mid-nineteenth century following the development of principal teachers. Educational administration was too important to be left to teachers to manage. People felt that leadership needed to be centralized. Superintendent of schools grew out of the terminology of the times.

Horace Mann saw the need for setting standards and for teachers to be educated. Teacher training schools were started in the nineteenth century. It was a new idea to train teachers formally. The purpose of these schools was to give teachers ideas they could use in their own way and assert their own individuality. These schools were often called Normal Schools. The reason for this name was because these teacher training schools were to establish standards, or norms. Prospective teachers were given courses in content knowledge and pedagogy, or instructional methods. They also were required to practice teach in a model school. Massachusetts developed a strong system of state supported common schools, which in turn became a model for the rest of the United States. The first Normal School for teacher training was established in Massachusetts in 1839.

An explosive growth in American schools occurred by the end of the nineteenth century. Public school enrollment increased from 7.6 million in 1870 to 12.7 million in the same decade. Public school expenditures increased from $69 million in 1870 to $147 million in 1890. The United States was providing more schooling to more children than any other nation. However, not all children could attend public schools together. Many Native Americans were sent to special government schools, where they were forced to abandon tribal language, customs, and dress. African Americans faced the same exclusion. Many created their own schools. Despite poverty, African Americans contributed greatly to the development of common schools for black children.

In the late 1800s, the question of the purpose of the American high school was divided between two main philosophies. Traditional educators saw high school as an institution for college preparation. This philosophy divided students based on economic, social, and ethnic backgrounds. Others believed that the high school should serve more as a people's school and offer a range of practical courses. The National Education Association addressed this issue by appointing a Committee of Ten in 1892 to establish a standard curriculum. This committee was composed mainly of educators and was chaired by Charles Eliot, who was the president of Harvard University.

The Committee of Ten recommended eight years of elementary education and four years of secondary education. The committee contributed in liberalizing the high school by offering alternatives to the Latin and Greek classic curricula and the belief that the same subjects would be beneficial for all students. The goal of high school was to prepare all students to do well in life, contribute to students' well-being, contribute to the good of society, and to prepare some students for college.

One of the most influential pieces of legislation affecting higher education was signed into law by Abraham Lincoln. It was the Morrill Land Grant Act. This act was first discussed in 1848, proposed in 1857, and then resubmitted in 1862. Although the Morrill Land Grant Acts were not directly aimed at curriculum reform, their effect was strong. These acts, the first being the assignment of land, and the second being the appropriation of annual funds, were aimed at founding universities across the frontier. The land-grant universities were mandated to offer instruction and research in agricultural and mechanical areas that never before had a place in higher education.

Another act that was important in creating social mobility was the Homestead Act of 1862, which gave an applicant freehold title to 160 to 640 acres of undeveloped land outside of the original 13 colonies. This act was signed into law by President Abraham Lincoln on May 20, 1862. Eventually, 1.6 million homesteads were granted and 270,000,000 acres were privatized between 1862 and 1986.

The Freedmen's Bureau Bill, which created the Freedmen's Bureau, was initiated by President Lincoln. The bill was passed in 1865 by Congress to aid former slaves through education, health care, and employment. The Bureau was part of the United States Department of War and was headed by Union Army General Oliver O. Howard. At the end of the war, the Bureau mainly provided emergency food, housing, and medical aid to refugees. Later, it focused on helping the freedmen adjust to being free. The main job of the Bureau was to set up work opportunities and supervise labor contracts. Former Confederate leaders soon attacked the Bureau for organizing African Americans against their former employers.

The most widely recognized accomplishments of the Freedmen Bureau are in the field of education. Overall, the Bureau spent five million dollars to set up schools for African Americans. By the end of 1865, more than 90,000 former slaves were enrolled as students in public schools. Under the direction of the Bureau, an estimated 25 institutions of higher learning for black youth were established by the time of its termination in 1872.

CHAPTER 4

CURRICULUM IN THE TWENTIETH CENTURY

At the beginning of the 20th century, parents and the general public would begin to demand more practical and useful curriculums. By 1900, the United States was becoming increasingly urban. Cities were crowded with immigrants arriving from all parts of the world. Between 1890 and 1930, over 22 million came to the United States, which included almost three million children. For these immigrants, school was the place where the American dream was nurtured, and the future took shape.

Up to this time, most education was centered on subject matter to be learned, with little or no consideration given to the learner. The twentieth century was more centered on the discovery of the child. After the Civil War, educational theories from Europe that emphasized the importance of the learner began to infiltrate American educational thought and practice. These ideas started the progressive education movement of the twentieth century.

With the Industrial Revolution came a dramatic increase in knowledge, particularly in the sciences. By the time of World War I, the physical sciences, the life sciences, and the social sciences had taken center stage. The demands of industry, business, agriculture, and the schools had produced new stores of knowledge in areas classified as the applied sciences.

The twin progressive aims of individual development and democratic group participation gained more attention as the twentieth century progressed. The older aim of individual success, brought about by the masses of immigrants, received growing attention during the early decades of the twentieth century. Because schooling was viewed as the way children gained material and social success, certain subjects of the curriculum were viewed in terms of their practical and cultural benefits. It was largely literacy, moral character development, and mental discipline that determined the elementary curriculum at this time.

Reorganization of the traditional subjects, as well as the addition of some new ones, occurred as a result of progressive pedagogical theories. Reading instruction in some schools came to be centered more on meaning rather than on rote memorization. Some arithmetic texts presented material in terms of practical problems instead of rules to be memorized. By the beginning of the twentieth century, history and literature were becoming important subjects in the upper grades of the elementary schools. The practical, progressive, and individual success aims motivated the introduction of subjects such as manual training, physical education, nature study, cooking, and sewing as the twentieth century progressed.

Around the turn of the twentieth century, scientific psychology and mental discipline began to slowly recede. About the same time, the vocational and technical aim of education began to gain in importance. Along with the vocational and technical aim, the aim of individual success, which served to support the cultural subjects as a way to upward social mobility was gaining in importance.

The twentieth century was a time of racial integration and school desegregation. In *Brown v. Board of Education of Topeka* in 1954, the Supreme Court ruled that racial segregation in public schools was unconstitutional. This case marked the beginning of a movement for civil rights and racial integration. The Civil Rights Act was passed by Congress in September of 1957. This act established a commission to investigate charges of the denial of voting rights and equal protection of the laws due to color, race, religion, or national origin. The Civil Rights Act of 1964 empowered the federal government to file school desegregation suits and to withhold federal funds from districts that practiced discrimination in federal programs.

Around the turn of the century, several national committees were appointed. Their reports had a significant and lasting effect on the secondary curriculum. From the time of the Civil War until the last decade of the nineteenth century, the high school curriculum had grown extensively. As a result, the high school curriculum represented a disordered array of courses. The curriculum was in need of order and standardization. This brought about the appointment of the Committee of Ten in 1892, which was chaired by Charles Eliot, president of Harvard. In its report issued one year later, the committee acknowledged the terminal as well as the college preparatory function of the high school. However, a curriculum entirely oriented toward the college-bound student was recommended. The committee recommended that terminal students be given the same program as those who were going to enter college.

A few months before the report from the Committee of Ten was issued, the Committee of Fifteen on Elementary Studies was appointed to determine whether the elementary course should remain at eight years or be shortened to six. At this time, American public schools had become standardized on the eight-year elementary and four-year secondary plan. The Committee of Ten raised questions about the feasibility of a satisfactory secondary school program limited to a period of four years. Some thoughts were expressed for beginning secondary education in the seventh instead of the ninth grade. Although the Committee of Fifteen recommended keeping the eight-year elementary and four-year secondary plan, it did call for closer articulation between the elementary and secondary school. The committee also called for some secondary subjects to be taught at the elementary level.

A third committee, the Committee of Thirteen on College Entrance Requirements, was brought about from the concern with standardization of college entrance requirements. Traditionally, entrance into a certain college was allowed after passing that college's entrance examinations. This committee proposed in its 1899 report that all candidates for college entrance be required to present evidence of having successfully completed four units of foreign language, two of mathematics, two of English, and one each of history and science, in addition to some acceptable electives. The Committee of Thirteen established the principle of college entrance based on units of high school work rather than examination. Also, this committee strongly recommended that the current eight-four organization be replaced by a six-six plan. Finally, in 1903, the National Education Association appointed a standing Committee on Economy of Time in Education. The reports of this committee, from 1903 to 1919, recommended that less time be given to elementary and more to secondary education. The committee was influential in fostering the curriculum changes that accompanied the development of the junior high school after 1910.

The Commission on the Reorganization of Secondary Education issued the Cardinal Principles of Secondary Education in 1918. The focus of this committee was to form objectives for secondary education. Changes were needed because of an increase in enrollment in secondary schools. The new focus would take into account individual differences, goals, attitudes, and abilities. The seven Cardinal Principles of Secondary Education are: health, command of fundamental processes, worthy home membership, vocation, civic education, worthy use of leisure, and ethical character. These seven principles are interrelated. In order for them to be successful, the student must be willing to follow the principles and have an ethical character that will allow learning to take place.

Perhaps the greatest influence on the elementary curriculum during the thirty years following World War I was the philosophy of progressivism. Only a small number of public schools actually implemented the progressive curriculum, but the idea was so widespread that the elementary curriculum was gradually transformed. A unique American conception of education was developed, particularly by John Dewey, who became the spokesperson for the movement. Progressive education is based on the ideal of a democratic society. It suggests that the learner's interests be taken into account. The learner and his experiences are most important in progressive curriculum making and teaching.

Although the older aims of literacy and character development remained in the elementary curriculum following World War I, the progressive education movement brought about a dramatic shift in focus. Literacy and character development in the progressive school were achieved through individual growth and the acquisition of democratic social skills and values. The vocational and mental discipline influence of the former period had virtually disappeared in the newer elementary schools. The separate subjects of reading, writing, spelling, and arithmetic were learned incidentally in progressive schools through participation in a variety of activities, such as sharing experiences with storybooks, writing and participating in dramatic presentations, taking field trips, and playing games. Greater emphasis on creative expression was achieved by including drawing, painting, music, dance, clay modeling, and craft work in the curriculum.

In many schools, the range of content was expanded greatly, while the number of subjects was reduced. For example, language arts was used to include a wide variety of activities involving reading, writing, speaking, and listening. Social studies included history, geography, economics, sociology, and civics. Science was used to designate study in the areas of biology, geology, physics, and chemistry. In all of these subjects, the achievement of the social competency aim was sought through the organization of cooperative group projects and activities. In physical education, emphasis was placed upon organized play and team games.

The new curricula shifted emphasis away from the mechanical ingestion of information to the understanding of information and the development of initiative, responsibility, critical thinking, cooperation, self-discipline, leadership, and problem-solving skills. Unfortunately, some of the schools were so child-centered that no prescribed curriculum was followed. The content and activities of the classroom were being determined almost entirely on the basis of the children's interests. The excesses and abuses of some progressivism educators, who really did not understand Dewey's philosophy, contributed to the decline of the progressive movement by the middle of the twentieth century. However, progressivism did a great deal to free the elementary curriculum of its formal character, to focus attention on children's needs and interests, to call into question the pedagogical legitimacy of a solely logical organization of subject matter, and to establish the experiential nature of the learning process.

In 1900, only about 10 percent of all high school aged youth were in secondary schools, with 75 percent of the graduates going on to college. By 1950, 85 percent of high school aged youth were in secondary schools, but only 25 percent of the graduates were going to college. The high school changed from primarily a college-preparatory institution for a select few to a comprehensive secondary school for all American youth.

The growing trend toward vocational education before World War I received momentum from the passing of the Smith-Hughes Act in 1917. This law provided federal funds for the salaries of teachers of agriculture, trades, industry, and home economics in secondary schools, and stipulated the vocational character of the courses to be taught. The act also provided for a federal board with the power of inspection and evaluation.

The junior high school developed rapidly during the 1920s. Grades seven, eight, and nine were usually housed in junior high school. Six major functions of the junior high school were: integration, exploration, guidance, differentiation, socialization, and articulation. Reflected in these functions are the progressive aims of individual development and democratic social competence.

Because it was a new institution which was unbound by tradition, the junior high school became a place for experimentation and originated a number of significant curriculum innovations. Separate subjects were correlated for an integration of knowledge, content and activities were related to life outside school, college-preparatory and vocational studies were avoided, resource and experience were employed in curriculum construction, and pupils shared in planning the learning activities in some classrooms.

The core curriculum consisted of some combination of English, social studies, and guidance at the junior high level. A longer block of time than the ordinary class period was usually allotted to the core. The homeroom teacher, usually responsible for the guidance of students in her homeroom, taught the course. The core curriculum was designed to integrate learning outcomes. By providing extended time periods, the teacher and students could work longer, which would improve interpersonal relations, personality development, and group problem-solving skills.

Industrial arts became a feature of the junior high curriculum to develop an interest in and an understanding of industrial processes. It was also designed to foster self-realization and develop practical skills in using common tools and machines. Offered in industrial arts were: home mechanics, woodworking, metal working, printing, and weaving. Home economics was regarded as the girls' counterpart of industrial arts for boys. However, by 1950, some schools were offering home economic for boys and industrial arts for girls. The aims of the courses were individual development and social competency in the home, family, and personal areas of life.

Health and physical education usually were required courses in junior high school. In the previous era, the program offered formal calisthenics. In the twentieth century, the program offered motor experiences, sports, and games.

Art and music in the junior high school were almost always offered. Painting and drawing, crafts, flower arrangement, picture framing and hanging, design and execution of school murals, and bulletin-board arrangement were some of the activities included in the art curriculum.

Grammar, rhetoric, spelling, speech, and literature frequently were combined as the language arts at the junior high level. The social studies usually combined the content of ancient history, world history, United States history, civics, economics, geography, and sometimes vocational guidance. In most schools, arithmetic and general mathematics were offered in the seventh and eighth grades, with quantitative aspects of home, business, and community problems. Banking, insurance, purchasing, and budgeting were used as ways to teach math. In many junior high schools, algebra was offered in the ninth grade for college-preparatory students, while general math or none at all was offered to the students who were not going to college. Science incorporated material from biology, physics, and chemistry. With the rise of the junior high school, foreign language study, formerly for the senior high grades, was often begun in the seventh grade. Most students did not begin the study of a foreign language until the ninth grade. The most common foreign languages offered were: Latin, Spanish, French, and German.

For the senior high school, some attention was given to progressive aims, but success in life was heavily focused on at this level. Success in American culture meant financial success; therefore, the high school diploma came to be sought for its cash value more than for any other reason. The fact that education was being assessed in terms of its cash value encouraged the comparison of schools to business corporations. Demands for the finest product at the lowest cost led to efficiency studies and the adoption of pseudoscientific business procedures in the operation of schools. Thus, educational and curriculum decisions were made on economic grounds or grounds that were not educational.

As nonacademic and vocational subjects began to enter the curriculum in the senior high school, new tracks appeared such as: commercial, industrial or manual arts, and agriculture. Gradually, the differentiated college preparatory curricula were replaced with a single college preparatory course. By the middle of the century, most high schools were operating on some variation of the tracking system that included differentiated curricula such as business or commercial, technical, general, vocational or industrial, agriculture, home economics, and fine arts, as well as the college preparatory course.

Although the high school housed all of its students under a single roof, they were separated according to their social-vocational prospects. The college-preparatory curriculum generally enrolled a middle- and upper-class clientele, while the vocational and industrial tracks mainly enrolled the lower- and lower-middle-class students. As the United States moved into being a credentialed society, the secondary school curriculum assumed an increasingly important role. Unfortunately, the role was in support of the status quo and social stratification.

The progressive education movement was still going fairly strong in the 1930s, although the social-vocational efficiency aim dominated the high school curriculum. Some high schools were implementing mainstream curricula designed for the individual and social development of all students. One of the main barriers to progressive curricula in most high schools, however, was college entrance requirements. There was the fear that excellence would be sacrificed if the requirements were removed. Arguments were that in an advanced technological society, the nation's leaders would have to come from the best colleges and universities, and that a stiff academic college preparatory curriculum was necessary for success in college. Therefore, out of this concern, the Progressive Education Association launched the Eight-Year Study.

From 1932 to 1940, the college performances of 1,475 graduates of thirty experimental secondary schools were compared with those of 1,475 graduates of traditional college-preparatory programs. Ralph Tyler, who was the director of evaluation, and his team had curriculum workshops for teachers. They also developed and put into action a number of innovative evaluation instruments. The results were that the graduates of the experimental schools did as well or better academically, socially, and psychologically as did those students who met traditional college entrance requirements.

In spite of the evidence from the Eight-Year Study, suggesting that a traditional college-preparatory curriculum might not be the only or the best way to prepare for college, the tradition continued. For most high school students aiming at college acceptance, the curriculum allowed for only minor variations of the following theme: three or four years of English, two to four years of mathematics, two to four years of foreign language, two to three years of social studies, and two to three years of science. Health and physical education were usually required. If students had the time, electives such as art, music, home economics, and personal typing could be taken. Noncollege-preparatory students who were enrolled in commercial, industrial, agriculture, and other curricula generally were taught English, mathematics, and science geared toward their lesser abilities.

Following World War II, the Cold War generated a great deal of anticommunist feelings and a fear of communist world power that caused some paranoia. With international threat, the progressive aims of individual development and democratic social competence seemed inappropriate to many people. Progressive curricula were attacked for their soft pedagogy and quackery. A tough, no-nonsense curriculum was felt to be needed that would ensure national leadership and survival in a hostile and competitive world.

Progressive education had critics that argued that the purpose of education was to cultivate intellectual skills and knowledge. Essentialist educators believed that schools should systematically train children in reading, writing, arithmetic, history, English, and foreign languages. Essentialists believed that schools should stress discipline and hard work.

The Progressive Education Association disbanded in 1956. The Soviet Union launched Sputnik I a year later, which achieved initial victory over the United States in the race for space and challenged American supremacy. These events signaled the eclipse of progressive tendencies in American curriculum development and marked the triumph of the social-vocational motive. During the next ten years, the discipline-centered curriculum became the means to develop human resources to serve the threatened Americans.

The discipline-centered curriculum was aimed at producing individuals who would perform competently in the present society. Highly trained leaders, scientists, and technicians were needed to meet the challenge of the world conditions. The emphasis in the discipline-centered curriculum was on training the elite and rigorous preparation for college. Elementary schools abandoned the progressive, self-contained classroom with a single teacher in favor of instruction by multiple teachers, each of whom was a specialist in science, mathematics, English, or social studies. The discipline-centered curriculum was organized around the specialized disciplines of knowledge. Science was replaced by chemistry, physics, and biology. Social studies was replaced by history, economics, and sociology. English was replaced by grammar, composition, and literature. Curriculum construction proceeded by separate disciplines. University professors dominated in the prescription of the objectives, content, and methodology. This era saw new math and the new sciences.

The whole curriculum was conceived to be simply the sum of the individual disciplines. The progressive notions of integration of knowledge, the aesthetic dimension, and the whole child were dismissed as unimportant or irrelevant. However, some aspects of the progressive movement were evident in the new curricula. The disciplines were taught through discovery and problem solving. Student involvement and cognitive processes were emphasized over the passive memorization of content. The content centered on principles and concepts rather than on the factual fragments that characterized the subject-centered curriculum of the pre-World War era.

As the Cold War waned, a reaction set in against the social control represented in the discipline-centered curriculum. There was an intensifying awareness of America's poverty, racism, pollution, and the involvement in the Vietnam War. By the middle of the 1960s, attacks were being launched against the irrelevance and immorality of the discipline-centered curriculum. It was claimed that the curriculum was unrelated to life outside of school. Other criticisms were its inherent fragmentation of knowledge and the focus on college-bound students. Out of this reaction came the humanistic curriculum.

The humanistic curriculum advocated humanization of the goals, content, and learning activities of the curriculum. It emphasized individual development within the framework of democratic social structures. Content in the humanistic curriculum focused on man. It utilized social problems, human concerns, and other principles as centers for curriculum organization. In-depth study of specialized disciplines was provided for when individual interest turned in that direction. Learning activities in the humanistic curriculum took into account the cognitive, aesthetic, and personal relations dimensions of learning and recognized the inseparability of these dimensions of human experience. Proponents of the curriculum summed up the humanistic position as individual integrity within a community context. Many high schools were offering a number of new courses intended to provide multiple curricular options. Some new courses were: environmental studies, religious literature, psychology, anthropology, black studies, mass communications, radio, television, film, twentieth-century literature, and current events.

After 1970, the momentum toward a more humanistic curriculum slowed. National enthusiasm for social reform ebbed, and was replaced by a mood of reassessment and consolidation. There was a need for order and the status quo. A reassertion of the business-efficiency movement in curriculum was evident. The evidence of this curriculum development was shown by the emphasis on behavioral objectives, accountability, national assessment, performance contracting, and performance-based curricula. However, the humanistic-progressive thrust continued to manifest itself with open education or the open classroom curricular concepts borrowed from the British primary school.

Open education included everything from classrooms without walls to a curriculum of learner choice. The idea was to allow students to choose their own course of study and to pursue those things that interested them most. The teacher's role was to facilitate and guide student learning. Articles began to be written in the 1970s pointing out that open schools were mainly places where students learned little of lasting importance. It was thought to be an experiment that had failed.

Curriculum reform has been mandated by various groups, such as the National Commission on Excellence in Education. Higher standards, more time on task, extended school day and year, increased homework, more rigorous academic courses, and better teacher preparation are some of the proposals that have been made by these groups.

Since the 1940s, there has been a dramatic increase in access to higher education for Americans. From the Servicemen's Readjustment Act of 1944 (GI Bill), which was signed into law by President Franklin D. Roosevelt, on up to the distance education movement of the 1990s, education has become available to a wider range of people, including women and minorities. No longer is higher education only for the white male.

The GI Bill made the government liable for a huge financial burden if many veterans took advantage of the benefits. Therefore, many people opposed the bill. More than half of eligible veterans took advantage of the education and training, and 2.2 million attended college. There was a reported cost of between $5.5 and $14.5 billion to the federal government. College enrollment increased dramatically and veterans made up more than 49% of the college population in 1947.

College enrollment doubled in the 1960s. Debates over the sort of knowledge that was most valuable took place. There were disagreements about the rigid curriculum on campuses which turned into student demonstrations. A number of colleges did away with their general education requirements because of their content, structure, or any other reasons that caused the demonstrations. New courses were started on minority and women's studies. Colleges were striving for a more flexible and broader curriculum that attended to the needs of individual students. Interaction between professors and students changed, and colleges began involving students more in learning and making curriculum decisions.

Junior colleges, or community colleges, were established in the twentieth century. These colleges allowed those who could not afford to attend college full-time, or who did not have the time due to families, to complete their course of study while working or at a reasonable pace. Community colleges offered a college-level curriculum with a vocational focus. These courses of study could be completed within two years. After those two years, students could transfer to four-year universities if they wanted to earn a bachelor's degree or beyond.

The funding of education for the poor began in this century. Scholarships for higher education were a product of the New Deal, which was the name that President Franklin D. Roosevelt gave to a series of economic programs that he initiated. This new idea of education for the poor was revolutionary.

Federal aid to public schools marks the first real involvement of the federal government with lower education. The federal act, PL 94-142, mandated that additional resources be provided for education of special students. With this act, our school systems are required to provide free, appropriate education to all children with disabilities with the least restriction possible. Public Law 94-142 was originally passed in 1975, and has been amended several times.

The computer was a huge advancement in this century. It has changed the way that people communicate, work, and learn. In the 1980s, the Internet made it possible to communicate with people thousands of miles away. This invention made our world truly global. Students are able to compete with others all around the world.

The surge of interest to better the American curriculum was increased in the twentieth century. The professionalism and specialization of higher education and the technology training and interest in foreign issues are trademarks of this period. The Greek and Latin debates of the previous century were no longer an issue. Educators and common citizens were more concerned with aligning the purpose of education with the changing needs of the world.

CHAPTER 5

CURRICULUM IN THE TWENTY-FIRST CENTURY

In the twenty-first century, there has been a national consensus that stresses the need for a system of accountability in the reporting of school, district, and state performance; increased parental choice; school-based management; and alternative certification for teachers. Shortly after the publication of *A Nation at Risk* in 1983, the National Governor's Association created seven task forces to study and report on education reform. The movement to develop national standards and national tests started during the Bush administration. The Republican party had been traditionally reluctant to expand the federal role in education. However, the Democrats saw the federal government as the primary guarantor of equity for disadvantaged students. The Bush administration persuaded Congress to establish the National Council on Education Standards and Testing. A major obstacle arose when the committee faced the issue of choice. America 2000 asked for several hundreds of millions of dollars to encourage states and school districts to offer programs to parents so that they could choose the public or private school they wanted their children to attend. During the last full year of the Bush administration, which was a presidential election year, no education legislation was enacted.

Congress passed President Clinton's Goals 2000: Educate America Act in March of 1994. This set the stage for the creation and certification of national curriculum standards. Goals 2000 proved to be controversial from the start. Many people felt that it was an intrusion of the federal government into state and local matters. The promotion of national standards addressed the issues of accountability, which shifted the public policy debate away from the distribution of resources in and out of schools towards measurable assessments justifying the distribution of rewards and punishments to schools and educators.

The Educate America Act created a new federal agency, the National Education Standards and Improvement Council (NESIC), which was responsible for certifying voluntary national content and performance standards; voluntary national opportunity-to-learn standards; and state standards for content, performance, and opportunity-to-learn, as well as state assessments. NESIC was supposed to ensure that national standards are internationally competitive and that state standards are comparable or higher in quality to the national standards. NESIC was to be representative in terms of race, ethnicity, gender, and disability characteristics. At least one-third of its nineteen members were to have experience in dealing with the needs of low-income, minority, limited-English-speaking, and handicapped children.

The National Education Goals are: ready to learn; school completion; student achievement and citizenship; teacher education and professional development; mathematics and science; adult literacy and lifelong learning; safe, disciplined, and alcohol- and drug-free schools; and parental participation. Goals 2000 also established a grant program to enable states to design their own reform plans. The law made no provision for national testing and prohibited the use of federally funded state tests for any decisions affecting students in the way of promotion or graduation.

Critics of Goals 2000 saw NESIC as a national school board that would have the power to interfere with state curricula. Opportunity-to-learn standards had always been the most controversial part of Goals 2000. Some educators worried whether national standards would narrow the curriculum to academic subjects. Others worried that NESIC might endorse low standards to achieve consensus, impose a politically biased national curriculum, and intrude into issues that belonged to the local and state levels. Goals 2000 seemed to not be understood and not discussed enough outside of Washington, D.C. In some communities, the critics of outcome-based education rejected the proposition that all children can learn, on grounds that the purpose was to dumb down the curriculum and hold back the brightest children until the slowest ones caught up with them.

In the United States, the term national curriculum is taboo. However, most states have developed curriculum guidelines to loosely govern their public schools. The state documents are mostly statements of broad goals. They are limited to content standards that are too general to provide real guidance to schools or parents. The statements are not specific enough to serve as functional guidelines for teaching and learning. In some states, work is being done to develop more specific statements that will apply across the state. All over the United States, committees of teachers, sometimes with parents and community members, are struggling with a task for which they have little support. They sometimes turn to the standards documents of the professional associations that are funded by the federal government.

The mention of national testing stirs uneasy feelings in students and educators alike. America has a love-hate relationship with tests. Testing is done in most domains of life. Surveys indicate widespread public support for more testing, even national testing. Americans' reliance on tests shows their faith in merit and opportunity.

Meanwhile, the idea of a new national test was winning more supporters. A White House advisory council made up of business and education leaders was considering that new national testing programs be established with federal leadership. The National Assessment of Educational Progress (NAEP) Governing Board recommended that the existing national assessment program, which had long provided achievement data for the whole country and was also beginning to furnish state-level results, should be changed to enable states and localities to use NAEP test instruments to appraise student performance at the level of school districts, schools, and individual students.

The idea of national testing failed because of five factors. The first factor being the crowd of people who dislike testing. The second being the conservatives who are fearful of federal control of education. Third are organizations with their own tests or plans for testing. They feel that national testing would threaten their status and revenues. Fourth are ill-informed policymakers. The fifth factor is a group of testing experts, whose technical requirements that any test must meet before it is used, tend to slow and complicate the process. Sometimes the requirements stop the testing altogether.

In matters of the curriculum, the federal role has been negligible by law and common agreement. Although many other nations have a national curriculum and national testing, education in the United States respects the principle of federalism. States have the primary responsibility for what is taught and tested in schools. However, in time, there is a possibility that the idea of national testing will reappear.

The federal No Child Left Behind Act (NCLB) of 2001 added new dimensions to the ongoing state efforts for improvement of student performance. NCLB focused public attention on the need for all students in all groups in all states to meet their state's proficiency standards in reading and mathematics by 2014. It spelled out requirements for assessment systems, teacher credentials, timetables for school improvement, and much more. With the 2014 NCLB deadline, states are working hard to meet the law's requirements and to sustain their previous efforts.

No Child Left Behind requires that schools assess at least 95 percent of students overall and in each subgroup. This law also requires states to provide information to the public on how schools are doing with all of their students. NCLB places responsibility on each state's policy-makers and education leaders to both sanction and assist certain schools that have failed to meet state-set criteria for two consecutive years. These schools, which are Title I schools, are the ones that receive federal funding to serve large percentages of students from low-income families.

Under NCLB, each state must determine whether schools, districts, and the state made adequate yearly progress (AYP) toward the goal that 100 percent of students meet or exceed state standards in reading and mathematics by 2014. Three components must be reported annually: the percentage of students participating in assessments; student performance in reading and mathematics; and student performance on other academic indicators. Other academic indicators are graduation and attendance rates. If one of the specified groups did not meet the annual target in reading or mathematics, it can still be considered to be making AYP if it both reduces the percentage previously not meeting the standard by 10 percent and meets its targets for the other academic indicators. This is called safe harbor. A school that does not make AYP for two consecutive years must be listed as a school in need of improvement. NCLB states that there be escalating consequences for each year that a Title I school or district remains on the needs-improvement list. To be removed from the list, a school or district must make AYP for two consecutive years.

The creation of improvement plans for low-performing schools and school districts is an important step in the intervention process. The process for creating and implementing these plans varies. Some schools or districts must create and implement their own plan. In other states, schools or districts implement improvement plans that are created by the state or another entity. Although the improvement planning varies from state to state, there are some constants. Improvement plans are blueprints for increasing the academic health of individual schools or districts. Also, states usually require low-performing schools or districts to submit an improvement plan in order to receive additional funding from the state. These plans identify academic or systemic deficiencies and lay out an agenda for improvement. Problems of leadership or instruction are usually addressed. The use of data, student tracking systems, and set measurable outcomes for the school or district to meet are encouraged. If a school or district does not meet the goals laid out in the improvement plan, it is subject to sanctions.

Sanctions and assistance increase if student performance continues to fall short of the state's standards. States that do not provide assistance to low-performing, Title I schools risk losing federal funding. Sanctions vary from state to state, but some are required by NCLB. Parents are given the option of transferring students from low-performing schools, tutoring and other supplemental academic services are offered, professional development for teachers is offered, restructuring schools is possible, and even taking over of school management.

Restructuring, which is also called reconstitution, sometimes involves creating a new philosophy, developing a new curriculum, hiring new staff, firing inadequate staff, and reducing teacher/student ratios. State and school officials cite the following problems as the basis for restructuring: low attendance and graduation rates; high dropout rates; poor performance on standardized tests, as well as a failure to show significant improvement in performance; poor morale among school community members; and deteriorating school buildings. Before such a dramatic action, the state notifies the school of their poor student performance. After a given time period, if the school fails to improve, the state or school district steps in and restructures. Displaced teachers and principals sometimes may reapply for their old jobs, but they and other candidates have to accept the new philosophy at the school in order to be hired.

In a state takeover, according to the Education Commission of the States (2004), the state legislature, the state board of education, or a federal court charges the state department of education or another designated entity, such as a mayor, with managing a school district. Many state policies provide a succession of sanctions for academic problems, with takeovers as the ultimate sanction. Other state policies target a single troubled school district for an immediate state takeover. The level of state control and influence in takeovers varies from state to state.

There is limited research on the effects of state takeovers. Student achievement still often falls short of expectations after a state takeover. Academic results tend to be mixed, with increases in student performance in some areas and decreases in other areas. For the most part, state takeovers have not produced dramatic and consistent increases in student performance.

In the higher education realm, distance education is shaping new debates. Students across race, gender, age, occupation, and level of competence are being able to obtain a college degree without ever leaving home. No longer will the convenient location of community colleges or universities be enough for some students to want to attend. Many institutions do not fully embrace the idea of earning a college degree solely using the Internet. The opponents of virtual universities, such as the University of Phoenix, are drawing attention to the fact that there needs to be a control of standards and modality for these online universities. Accreditation is the topic of their debates. Opponents argue that the process through which instruction takes place and the way that practices are monitored at these facilities is questionable. Many educators will continue to be suspicious of the curriculum and delivery of instruction of distance education programs. Instruction in colleges may be conducted increasingly through a computer monitor instead of the traditional face-to-face instruction.

Curriculum for the twenty-first century must address the new needs of American students. The curriculum should be outcome-based; encourage critical thinking; be research-driven; include active and collaborative learning; be student-centered with the teacher being a facilitator or coach; be motivating; be integrated and interdisciplinary; use authentic assessment; be connected to students' interests and experiences; connect to the real world; use projects and multiple forms of media for learning and assessment; address student diversity; and use multiple literacies in order to align to living and working in a globalized world. The curriculum should not be textbook-driven, but include many other resources for learning. Knowledge should not be memorization of information, but should be constructed by research and application for today's world.

CHAPTER 6

CONCLUSION

The curriculum of American schools has always been dynamic, reflecting the ever-changing American society. Americans have looked to schools to prepare their children for the world. The forces that have made the nation so dynamic are still going strong; therefore, the need for curriculum change remains strong. The capitalistic market economy in the world produces a workplace that is constantly changing. The resulting insecurity motivates Americans to give their children a competitive edge. Many Americans believe that their children could compete better in today's society if schools raised their academic standards.

America now faces new challenges. The divorce rate has risen, and fewer children live with a stable nuclear family throughout their school years. Even in families with both parents at home, both parents usually work, which leaves little time for their children. Many children spend more time with television, computers, and video games than at school or with parents. Information and communication technologies have grown dramatically in recent decades. Some wonder if schools should ignore this technology or adapt to it.

Today, the foundations of schooling face the greatest challenges since the creation of public school systems. Many Americans want to end the public school's monopoly in order to open the way for different kinds of schools to compete for attendance. Charter schools, home schooling, and proposals to issue government vouchers to students for tuition at non-public schools reflect this desire.

Historically, Americans have embraced change. Change meant progress. If this traditional view remains, America should expect a great deal of innovation. However, many Americans today fear change. Economic change has brought the loss of jobs and industries. Americans have suffered from the trauma of broken families. They have struggled to keep families intact when both parents work outside the home. Americans have fought to maintain businesses in the face of global competition. Environmental degradation, pollution, and global warming are some fears of today. The war on terrorism and its catastrophic effects has many Americans afraid. Scandals have undermined faith in the government. However, innovation was once the genius of the American society. Demands are stressful, but they can also energize. There must be collaboration in our school systems. Working together not only strengthens personal bonds, but infuses educators with new enthusiasm about their job. A sense of vision and purpose about education strengthens educators' engagement with the school and community.

As past research shows, educational reform is an ongoing process and seemingly never complete. It requires major commitment over a long period of time. Curriculum reform efforts should not be mere reactions to the excesses of a previous era of reform, but should begin as an attempt to solve a problem. In working on a problem, one must see what happened before. Our strength lies in our experience. Our misfortune lies in our failure to use it. American schools will not be truly successful until we accept the fact that in a world of change, schools and practices will be constantly evolving. A whole new approach is needed that makes change our friend. We study the history of education to help us study its future. It is difficult to know where we are going if we do not know where we have been. John Dewey said, "We do not merely have to repeat the past. We use our past experiences to construct new and better ones in the future."

References

Campbell, R. F., Fleming, T., Newell, L. J., & Bennion, J. W. (1987). *A history of thought and practice in educational administration.* New York, NY: Teachers College Press.

Cremin, L. A. (1997). *ASHE reader on the history of higher education,* pp. 315-317. New York: Simon & Schuster.

Diaz, A. & Lord, J. (2005). *Focusing on student performance through accountability.* Atlanta, GA: Southern Regional Education Board. Retrieved from http://www.sreb.org/main/ Goals/ Publications/05E05-Accountability.pdf.

Drake, W. E.(1955). *The American school in transition.* New York, NY: Prentice-Hall, Inc.

Education Commission of the States. (2004). *State takeovers and reconstitutions.* Retrieved

January 12, 2007 from http://www.ecs.org/ clearinghouse/51/67/5167.htm.

Ellis, A. K. (2004). *Exemplars of curriculum theory.* Larchmont, NY: Eye on Education, Inc.

Finn, C. E. (1991). *We must take charge: Our schools and our future.* New York, NY: Maxwell Macmillan International.

Goldman, S. (1966). *The school principal.* New York: The Center for Applied Research in Education.

Gutek, G. L. (1983). Education and schooling in America. Englewood Cliffs, NJ: Prentice-Hall, Inc.

Jennings, J. F. (1998). *Why national standards and tests: Politics and the quest for better schools.* Thousand Oaks, CA: Sage Publications, Inc.

Kiester, E. (1994). The G.I. Bill may be the best deal ever made by Uncle Sam. *Smithsonian.* Washington, D. C.: Smithsonian Institute.

Klein, M. F. (1989). *Curriculum reform in the elementary school: Creating your own agenda.* New York, NY: Teachers College Press.

Kowalski, T. J. (2004). *Public relations in schools.* Upper Saddle River, NJ: Pearson Education, Inc.

Kraus, J. W. (1961, June). The development of a curriculum in the early American colleges. *History of Education Quarterly 1,* 64-76.

Krueger, C. (2002). *State interventions in low-performing schools and school districts.* Denver, CO: Education Commission of the States.

Lucas, C. J. (1994). *American higher education: A history.* New York: St. Martin's Griffin.

Marshall, J. D., Sears, J. T., Allen, L. A., Roberts, P. A., & Schubert, W. H. (2007). *Turning points in curriculum: A contemporary American memoir.* Upper Saddle River, NJ: Pearson Education, Inc.

Mondale, S. & Patton, S. B. (2001). *School: The story of American public education.* Boston, MA: Beacon Press.

Ornstein, A. C. & Levine, D. U. (1993). *Foundations of education.* Boston, MA: Houghton Mifflin Company.

Perley, J. & Tanguay, D. M. (1999, October 29). Accrediting on-line institutions diminishes higher education. *The Chronicle of Higher Education,* p. B4.

Pulliam, J. D. & Van Patten, J. J. (1999). *History of education in America.* Columbus, OH: Merrill.

Raubinger, F. M. (1969). *The development of secondary education.* New York, NY: Macmillan.

Rudolph, F. (1990). *The American college & university: A history.* Athens, GA: The University of Georgia Press.

Sarason, S. B. (1996). *Revisiting the culture of the school and the problem of change.* New York, NY: Teachers Press College.

Tanner, L. N. (1983, November). Curriculum history and educational leadership. *Educational Leadership, 41(3)* 38-42.

Walker, D. F. & Soltis, J. F. (2004). *Curriculum and aims.* New York, NY: Teachers College Press.

Williams, B. (2003). *Closing the achievement gap: A vision for changing beliefs and practices.* Alexandria, VA: Association for Supervision and Curriculum Development.

Williams, R. L. (1997). The origins of federal support for higher education. *ASHE reader on the history of higher education,* pp.267-272. New York: Simon & Schuster.

Zais, R. S. (1976). *Curriculum principles and foundations.* New York, NY: Thomas Y. Crowell Company, Inc.

Made in the USA
Middletown, DE
17 May 2022

65880139R00043